DESTINATION
TRANSFORMATION

Your Navigational Roadmap
to a Totally Fulfilling, Pretty
Amazing, Completely
Rewarding Dream Life

Dr. LaVerne Adams

ISBN # 978-0-9848567-6-3

Copyright 2015 - Registration number TXu 1-965-040

Destination: TRANSFORMATION - Your Navigational
Guide to a Totally Fulfilling, Pretty Amazing, Completely
Rewarding Dream Life eCourse Workbook

⊕→ Dedication

This book is dedicated to Dr. Gladys West, one of the inventors of the Global Positioning System (GPS). Her insight helps us to dream beyond where we are right now and get directions to where we want to be.

And to all of my sensational clients who have taken full advantage of the powerful opportunity to use my coaching to totally transform your life. You understand the tremendous value of having a coach to get more done in the least amount of time. I am humbled by your accolades that are an affirmation of my gift and the remarkable results I see in your lives. You are a living testament that it can be done and are living proof of the fulfillment of my purpose for being on the planet!

Destination: TRANSFORMATION - Your Navigational Guide

to a Totally Fulfilling, Pretty Amazing,

Completely Rewarding Dream Life

This book is very effective tool to totally transform every area of your life. Be sure to look for other tools designed to completely change your life. You will never be the same!

This book is also the workbook companion of the online Destination Transformation video eCourse that can be found at:

DestinationTrasformation eCourse

⊙→ Foreword

"Each individual has a life journey. When you look within yourself, you will understand the journey is not one that we choose. A path that is ordained or predestined that is out of our control. We at times think that we control our own fate, and that is the biggest lie we tell ourselves.

Do not change who you are. This is when life begins to bloom for you. It is that blossom that creates energy, knowledge, wisdom, and peace that every human yearns for. Be patient as patience is a virtue. Seasons change, so create a narrative that forever fulfills the best part of you. Focus on the thoughts, ideas, and desires that will transform your life.

What Dr. LaVerne Adams has done in this book is to present a vehicle to help you focus, prepare, and upgrade your existence so that you can live the life you dream. Let's spring into a new beginning to upgrade yourself and prepare to be great! YOU HAVE SOMETHING SPECIAL! YOU HAVE GREATNESS IN YOU!

~ Les Brown

⊙→ Contents

Navigational Direction 1 **The Road to Review Your Life**.............. 9

Navigational Direction 2 **The Road to Your Rediscovery**...........15

Navigational Direction 3 **The Road to Your Revelation**.............22

Navigational Direction 4 **The Road to Your Renewal** 29

Navigational Direction 5 **The Road to Your Reinvention**...........37

Navigational Direction 6 **The Road to Your Responsibility** 44

Navigational Direction 7 **The Road to Your Reason**.....................50

Navigational Direction 8 **The Road To Your Relationships**.......57

Navigational Direction 9 **The Road to Your Results**....................65

Navigational Direction 10 **The Road to Your Reflection** 73

Navigational Direction 11 **The Road to Your Revolution**..........81

Navigational Direction 12 **The Road to Your Reward**.................88

⟳ Navigational Direction 1

↱ The Road to Review Your Life

> *Too many of us are not living our dreams*
> *because we are living our fears" Les Brown*

Welcome to the first session of Destination: TRANSFORMATION. I'm Dr. LaVerne Adams, your navigational guide to a Totally Fulfilling, Pretty Amazing, Completely Rewarding Dream Life.

In this first session I will help you to better understand where you are and how you got there. And I will help you uncover the source of some recurring themes that you experience that continue to block your progress in life. When we are done, you will know how to turn negative themes into positive tools that will greatly advance your life.

I can help you because I have overcome numerous obstacles in my own life because I discovered the directions needed for a dynamic change. It might interest you to know that although I was born a triplet, the triple threat of poverty, lack, and homelessness was our reality because my mother lost her job when her boss found out she was pregnant, and consequently she lost her apartment because she couldn't pay her rent. Therefore, when we were born, she asked the hospital if we could stay there until she found us a home. Fortunately, our grandparents stepped in to support our family but that was not the best scenario because they had an abusive relationship.

And, if that wasn't enough, I suffered from a devastating divorce after a 25-year marriage, losing absolutely everything I held near and dear, finding myself once again in poverty, lack and home-lessness as a result. But by the grace of God, I was able to turn my life around, and now I am an author, community leader, spir-itual teacher and transformational leadership consultant. This is because I did the hard work necessary to totally transform my life, and now my entire mission is to support people just like you, to do exactly the same...

In this session I am going to help you think about where your life began, and what may still be influencing you right now. You will learn how to strategically review your life so you can shift to get the outcomes you desire.

There were particular dynamics that took place the day you were born that you had absolutely no control over. You did not choose the day, or the hour, or the place where you were born, or choose who your parents would be. You come to realize that there was so much that you had absolutely nothing to do with. But all of these factors and experiences had a dynamic impact on who you are today because you continue to rehearse the script.

This is important information when determining where you are today. All of the parameters around your birth make you distinctly different than anyone else. Just look on the tips of your fingers to see that you were imprinted with a distinctive and unique des-tiny. Whether it was a proud or a sad moment when the doctor announced your entrance into the world...there is no one who is exactly like you...You have a very special purpose for being alive.

The first step on the Road to Reviewing your life is to take an honest assessment of where you have been. Think about the things that surrounded your birth...good and bad or indifferent. Be honest in your assessment about how those circumstances could have shaped your life. For example, if you were born into poverty. This will affect the way you view and use money. This experience could also have an impact on your self-esteem and how you view others....It has been said that *"You cannot know where you are going if you don't know where you've been."*

And if you don't know where you are going in life, how will you know when you get there? When you take stock of our journey through life so far, you can learn some very important and revealing clues.

A technique that you can use to better understand where your life is right now is to begin to look for patterns and recurring themes that continue to appear as a result of your past. Understand that you cannot change the past, but you can be intentional about what you want to see in your future.

REVIEW YOUR LIFE TECHNIQUE

- Have you ever said, why does this keep happening to me?

- What are the recurring scenarios that continue to happen over and over?

- Do you continue to rehearse the same script of your life, only with different players?

I used this technique of reviewing my own life and I saw a recurring theme of continuous abandonment from people to whom I gave my absolute trust. As a result, I learned to put the necessary boundaries in place to keep me from setting myself up to be in abusive relationships over and over again.

Think honestly about how good and bad experiences could have shaped your thinking and behaviors. You have the power to accentuate the good and transform the bad in your life. We must be intentional to learn something positive from our negative experiences.

Now, you might be saying that you do not feel powerful right now. I want you to understand that the negative things you may be experiencing are not an indicator to where your life is headed. This is important information to assess where you have been. Then, use it to inform where you need to be.

Now think about what changes you would like to see in your life. You can rewrite your story with a good ending no matter how bad things have been. Using this technique is the first step to totally transform your life.

Only you have the power to transform the shortcomings of your past. You can make adjustments. See in your mind what you wanted to happen differently. See the best possible outcomes! Use your power to change your outcomes to look more like what you want to see. Keep trying till you get it right!

I developed this course to help you to discover the power you have to create a pretty awesome life. I believe that when you were created, God had a dream about how awesome your life could be.

What you have learned in this session will help to move you forward on your journey to have a totally transformed life. You are well on your way to a totally fulfilling, pretty amazing, completely rewarding dream life. Be sure to use this DESTINATION TRANSFORMATION workbook to chart your progress.

NAVIGATE YOUR LIFE

Decoding your destiny is critical to interpret the destiny clues that your life is giving you. Your life will be literally transformed as you begin to make sense out of why and where you are right now. Make a real commitment to determine the direction that your life needs to take and honestly answer the following questions about where you are on your life's journey:

1. What is the one thing that you have learned about yourself from this session?

2. What are the recurring obstacles that keep you from living your dream?

3. What things do you need to do to overcome these obstacles?

4. What one thing will you do to be more conscious and aware of how your past is still affecting your present?

5. Think about the things that keep you stuck. What are some action steps will you take to change your future and get unstuck?

6. Which behaviors do you need to change to see the outcomes you desire?

7. What do you need to do to get out of your own way to move forward?

8. What evidence will you see when you get where you want to be?

9. How long do you think it will it take for you to implement these new behaviors?

Now you know how necessary it is to get on the road to review your life so that you can discover the recurring themes you see in your life so that you can address them head on.

UP NEXT... Our next turn is onto the Road to Rediscovery.

The Road to Your Rediscovery

> *Life has no limitations except the ones you make*
> *– Les Brown*

In this session I will share the ride with you and show you the value of tapping into your dreams as a way to live a more fulfilled life. I will help you discover how vital it is to renew your sense of wonder.

You will find out what you need to know to move forward successfully with clarity, insight, and vision. You will learn how to change your attitude and ultimately change your future. First answer these questions:

- Is your life stagnant?

- Do your current life activities broaden or limit you?

- Are you ready for a fresh wind of enthusiasm to blow through your life?

You cannot teach a man anything; you can only help him discover it in himself. **—Galileo Galilei**

Life becomes drab when you lose your sense of wonder. One of the most vital gifts that you can have in life is a sense of awe to make life deeply meaningful. From the time you were born, you went through a series of moments of discovery. When you were young, you were free to let your imagination soar! These moments helped to shape you and brought interest into your life.

As you got older, you became less imaginative because one day the unimaginable happened. Life takes an unexpected turn and you found yourself disillusioned. You may have even subconsciously discontinued your journey of discovery and focused upon coping and survival strategies. Then, if you stayed in this position too long, you ended up in the danger zone where life became dissatisfying, dull, and dreary.

Then there are circumstances that are beyond your control that can cause you to get stuck in dysfunctional vicious cycles, like a bad marriage, or the unexpected death of a loved one. When you can't seem to find your way out, you lose the ability to envision a bright future for yourself. The solution for this issue can be found in a rediscovery.

I remember the moment that my life went down the tubes...My marriage fell apart. I lost my job and my home. I had gotten so low that I could not see a future for myself. I could no longer believe that I had a destiny. Then one day the light came on. I got an epiphany that shifted the course of my life. I got a coach who helped me realize that as long as I kept focusing on my problem, it would grow bigger. I discovered that I needed to refocus on the dream that I wanted to see come to pass in my life if I wanted to see change in my life.

In order to live a vibrant life and fulfill your destiny, you must once again enter this realm of rediscovery. You must ignite the power to dream a dream that will pull you out of the pit that you find yourself. But you might ask: "How can I do this in the case when my morale has fallen to an all-time low? When are things going so wrong that it seems impossible to dream?" When there seems to be no end in sight?

This may occur as a result of traumatic circumstances. There are many factors that causes you to feel connected to people, places, and things that you know are not good for you. You subconsciously organize your life around the familiar. Regardless of how dysfunctional things have become, you sense the illusion of stability. You feel compelled to maintain the status quo because it gives you a false sense of security. This becomes especially problematic when you lock yourself into a protective comfort zone. This is one of the reasons why we can go to great lengths to protect toxic environments and relationships. Although it may not be all we want, it is all we know, and we stay in survival mode. But if you stay there, you will never realize your dreams. This may be difficult because trauma has a way of giving you amnesia and can cause us to forget the pain and we stay in a vicious cycle.

Your dreams are the gateway to your future. This is as simple as remembering what you dreamed about being when you were a child. If you want to live a satisfying life, you must always keep your dreams in the forefront of your mind. You must make a conscious decision to be willing to do whatever it takes to shift out of this dangerous zone! The first step out is to reclaim your dreams. You must be intentional about rediscovering what makes your heart smile.

Oprah Winfrey once said that *"The greatest discovery of all time is that a person can change his future by merely changing his attitude."*

If you change your attitude, you can change your life. One way to do this is to be aware that some of your behaviors have become dysfunctional. These are the behaviors that tend to keep you stuck in unhealthy emotional environments. If you can see your crisis as the catalyst to move you from your place of complacency, these life-changing experiences could catapult you into an entirely new way of being.

Sometimes crisis brings us to the reality of just how desperate our lives have become. If we allow it, crisis can become the turning point by which to shift into the greatest moments of our lives. This shift can help to better align us with our dreams.

There are a few things that you can do to see lasting change in the way you think. You first need to understand that if you want to see something different, you need to do something different. It takes enormous courage to leave everything you know, but you can do it!

You must be willing to take the risk and go out into the unknown of where you have never been in order to find fulfillment. These new experiences will recreate the sense of wonder you need to move forward. If you are unwilling to move out, you may always be stuck between dissatisfaction and frustration. You have to make the hard choice to move from where you are to get to where you want to be.

It is times like these that we most need the insight, direction, and encouragement to take action. This course was designed to give you the sense of direction you need to transform your life. Be encouraged! You are not alone. I am here to help guide you through a series of transformative experiences. There are a few things that you can do to be more intentional about reawakening your dreams. Here are techniques that you can use to rediscover your dreams and see a transformed life:

- Get out of your comfort zone and be inquisitive.

- Be adventurous!

- Within the next week, try a new food item.

- Within the next month, experience a new culture or ethnic group.

- Listen to different types of music.

- This year, make friends with someone less fortunate.

As you do, you will begin to discover that your child-like sense of wonder will return. You will begin to appreciate the little things and feel a deeper sense of meaning in life. These experiences will enrich your life. You will feel more fulfilled. Then, everything else in life will become more satisfying. Now you are on your way to seeing total transformation! Oprah Winfrey *said that "The greatest discovery of all time is that a person can change his future by merely changing his attitude."*

What you have learned about reigniting your dream, will help to move you forward on your journey to totally transform your life. You are well on your way. Let's continue our journey together. Be sure to use this DESTINATION TRANSFORMATION workbook to chart your progress.

NAVIGATE YOUR REDISCOVERY

As you go through this dimension of rediscovery there are many things that you will begin to recall about yourself that you may have forgotten. As you attempt to remember your dreams, you will be reminded of what is really important to you. Write these things down. You will need this information when you start to feel like losing hope. These dreams will help to keep you focused. These are your dreams. Own them!

Honestly answer the following questions about where you are with your self-discovery:

1. How will you nurture your dreams now that you know how important they are to your future?

2. Have you discovered anything new or different about yourself lately?

3. What situation or experience brought about this newness?

4. Was this a change that was beneficial for you? How?/How not?

5. Are you struggling with something in your life that you know needs to be changed because it keeps you from fulfilling your dreams? What is it?

6. What would happen if your dreams and goals were realized today? What steps will you take to get there?

7. List 3 things that you will do to reignite your sense of wonder.

UP NEXT...

On our next turn, we will look at The Road to your Revelation...

Navigational Direction 3

The Road to Your Revelation

> *You are the only real obstacle in your*
> *path to fulfilling it – Les Brown*

In this session I will show you how to realize some very revealing truths about yourself. You will learn why it is important to travel on the Road to Your Revelation if you want to see real changes in your life. I will also show you how to get revelation and why you need it. Then I will show you where to find revelation and what to do with the revelation once you receive it.

In this session I will show you how you can position yourself to get the revelation you need to see success in your life. I am sure that you can agree that it is the difficult times in life that reveal to us who we truly are. It is the trying circumstances that show us what we are really made of.

Getting a revelation is simply unknown information that is revealed to you by someone else. It can be an eye-opening truth that confirms what you already know, or it can completely surprise you.

Revelation is critical because it contains things that you need to know but are not aware of. It also contains the missing pieces that you need to move forward in life. Most times revelation comes from outside of you to stir up what is already inside of you.

As you go through this session, think about the last time something was revealed to you to help you change. This information may have been spoken to you, or it may have come through a still, small voice inside, or through someone else. Or maybe it could have been God by making an impression on your heart. Maybe you feel that you have never received a revelation.

Many times, it takes a challenging circumstance to show us who people really are. Real friends stick by you in good times and in bad. When things are going well, it seems like everyone is your friend. It is not until we get in a pinch that we recognize who is really there for us.

You may have made some very costly mistakes in life because of poor choices. These bad decisions have caused you to lose some pretty valuable things. But if you don't learn from your experiences, you will find yourself repeating the same mistakes over and over again. And, if you just don't know how to break free from a vicious cycle, you will be stuck or hit a wall in life, unable to move forward. When this happens, you are left with the feeling that there are no other options.

Another reason you may not know what to do is because you don't know who to ask. This is primarily because there is a shortage of people available who can give you the personal attention you need. Our dilemma is too often the people with whom you are closely associated are often suffering from similar experiences, or worse...If the people you associate with don't know how to solve their problems, how in the world can they help you with yours?

It is during these difficult times that you know you should seek assistance. But your pride may make you think that you should be able to figure things out on your own. But what would you say if I told you how easy it is to position yourself in a way that you could receive instructions every single day?

It really is quite simple, and I want to show you how you could you access the information you need. You could be in a position to receive revelation every day. Imagine never having to wonder what you should do or which direction to take. Imagine knowing with confidence the choices you should make to fulfill your dreams...

First it is critical to understand that your answer, your solution, is inside of you... Then you must find the right people to help draw it out of you. When you connect with the right people, they can help you bring it out of you. If you want to transform your life, it is critical for you use this technique to seek out mature stable people for their wisdom. Maintain connections with inspiring and well-adjusted people. The easiest way to bring these people into your life is to *serve* them.

This is the best way to position yourself for the revelation you need; put yourself right in the midst of it! Being in their presence, will naturally reveal life's deep secrets that will help you realize your destiny. These people are easy to recognize, but sometimes they intimidate you, so you keep our distance. They make you uncomfortable because you think that they have arrived and will reject you.

There are times when you miss the turn onto the Road to Revelation because the real issue is that sometimes you do not want to face your own inadequacies. Their truth can be too painful so you avoid them like the plague because you know that they will challenge you to be better, go further, and set higher expectations. Sometimes that is just too much work, so you resist.

Deep down in your heart, you know traveling this road would bring peace and wholeness into your life but because you are afraid, you make excuses for why you don't need to turn there. I've been there. But I am not sure where my life would be right now had it not been for the great people in my life people who helped me grow. These people helped to reveal valuable information that enabled me to move forward with my life. The truth is that you need people to help you. If you knew how to solve your problems, you would have done it by now.

When you make excuses, you can miss some very important messages that you desperately need to move forward and get unstuck in your life. You may even get distracted and off course by focusing on some of the following:

- Dates – You procrastinate and say you are waiting for a particular date. When you do this, you could miss out on divine timing.

- Late – You have a habit of being tardy and even lazy. You miss a moment because you are too tired doing unimportant things.

- Hate – You are envious or jealous of the status and blessings of others and miss your blessing by keeping your eyes on others.

- Wait – You make up an arbitrary reason that you are waiting for some special timing, but the truth is that you are simply afraid to move forward.

- Mate – You miss a revelation because you are depending upon someone else to validate when you can receive it.

- Rate – Sometimes you can berate yourself with feelings of unworthiness.

Regardless of where you are, one decision can change your life. Make up in your mind now that you are worthy of more. Open yourself up to receive the much-needed revelation that you need to change your life. The people, places and things you need will suddenly appear. Ask for wisdom and it will be given to you. Seek revelation and you will find it. Mabel Collins once said that "When the student is ready, the teacher appears.

What you have learned in this chapter will help to move you forward on your journey to totally transform your life. Get in the proximity of wise people and allow them to help you see for you what you cannot see for yourself. Be sure to use this DESTINATION TRANSFORMATION workbook to chart your progress.

NAVIGATE YOUR REVELATION

As you go through this dimension of revelation there are many things that you will discover about yourself that you may not have known.

Honestly answering the following questions about how revelation impacts your life:

1. Are you waiting for a special date or for all conditions to be perfect before you seek out those who can provide you with the revelation you need?

2. Is there is anyone you cannot go to for help due to envy or jealousy? Jealousy is a sign that you are not ready to move to the next dimension. How can you quickly overcome this obsession and move forward?

3. Are you often late and miss critical moments?

4. What are some of the things that you can do to break the habit of lateness and laziness that is keeping you from your fulfilling your destiny?

5. Which mate, partner, or friend are you waiting for before you can pursue the revelation you need to fulfill your destiny?

UP NEXT...

Our next turn is onto The Road to Your Renewal.

↱ The Road to Your Renewal

> *When your why is big enough, you will*
> *find your how – Les Brown*

Welcome to the fourth session of Destination: Transformation. In this session, I will show you a variety of ways how you can transform every area of your life through the process of renewal. I will also help you to raise your awareness of the necessity of renewal in your life.

I recognized the need for renewal when I began to feel burned out from my work. After doing what I am passionate about for years, which is helping and serving others, it began to take its toll on me. I no longer wanted to go to work. I started to have health issues, anger, and irritability problems. These were sure signs that I was experiencing fatigue and stress and it was imperative for me to change my routines.

As we prepare to go down this Road of Renewal, use this as your opportunity to think about some of your habits. Use this technique to begin your renewal process:

- Think about your habits and how long you have had them and how well they benefit you.

- Take time to think about all of your good habits.

- Honestly assess your diet, exercise, work habits, etc.

- Assess as many good habits as you can.

- Now think about some habits that you have that may not be so good for you.

- Properly assess how these habits are negatively impacting your lifestyle.

- Think about the process by which these habits have developed over time.

Use this information as you develop your renewal plan. Decide which area you want to change in your life. Make up your mind to start with one area at a time. This is the key to seeing a total transformation in every area of your life.

If you want to see transformation in every area of your life, you will need to work on each of the eight core areas in your life. These include your: mental, emotional, physical, spiritual, relational, financial, professional, and material.

Write SMART Goals that would help to guide you toward the change that you want to see. Remember, this is a process. It took time to get where you are today. It will take time to change.

Sometimes we view this vital renewal process as a luxury rather than a necessity. The good news is that it is never too late. We can reposition our lives to make old things feel like new again. All we have to do is activate the power we have within to renew.

You only have to look around to appreciate this powerful ability of regeneration with every season. Even nature contains within it the wisdom to know the time that it needs to replenish and renew itself. There are numerous plants and trees and animals that display this natural phenomenon.

Self-renewal is critical if you are to continue to move forward to living successful, fulfilling and meaningful lives. When you begin to see the renewal process as a necessity, you will find numerous opportunities to be refreshed in a multitude of ways. There are opportunities for renewal anytime and anywhere in our everyday lives. You simply need to recognize these valuable moments when they appear.

Although it all sounds good, sometimes you may want to keep things as comfortable as possible for as long as possible. Your subconscious mind gets easily fooled into a false sense of security, even though you know deep within that you are unfulfilled. It often takes the cataclysmic power of a crisis to pry you out of our place of contentment.

This is because you will subconsciously want to stay in your comfort zone. Although you know you need to change, you may have not been able to accomplish your goals. Sometimes we can be like fleas in a jar. We restrict ourselves to only what we are accustomed to and therefore never try to go higher than what has already been attempted. With each passing day, we have the phenomenal opportunity to strive to be better. For whatever reason, humankind has a tendency to resist this natural process of renewal although we know that it is good for us.

There is a quality of life that is often missed in life when you seek to maintain the status quo. Life becomes stale. You become less effective in our daily dealings and routine activities. It is the first major sign that your renewal process is long overdue. Personal crisis is your announcement that things need change in your life.

Crisis comes as a distinct opportunity to see life from a different vantage point to force us out of our comfort zone. It is at these times that we can experience life on a much deeper level. But, if you ignore this opportunity, you can get stuck in a rut and not even know how you got there. Sometimes it's not until you burn out that you realize that you need a renewal, and this crisis moment is only the tip of the iceberg.

It is during crisis moment that your body, your mind and your circumstances are all "screaming" that it is time to shift. During these times, you must learn to see yourself in a whole new way. And all too often we ignore the important signs like chest pains or ongoing headaches. And when you ignore the signs, you set yourself up for future disaster.

These warning signs may manifest as physical ailments or personal catastrophes. But it doesn't need to be this way. You can learn techniques to get in touch with yourself on a deeper level. You should always be on the lookout for opportunities to experience life in a new way. Accept the fact that you do not have all of the answers you need. Seek out the assistance you need to help you renew your body, soul and spirit because no matter how bad you want it, you may still need someone to be accountable to, who will support you in your journey.

Please feel free to take advantage of my coaching services, which are available to help you with this goal setting process. If you are having trouble with this part of the assignment, this is a great opportunity for you to get the support you need to set achievable goals that are based upon your needs and personality type. Please reach out to me at DrLaVerne@DrLaVerneAdams.com. I am here to support you on your journey toward renewal and transformation. I know how difficult this can be to accomplish alone. I offer my assistance because I understand that change is not an easy thing to do alone.

You should always be in search of information that will improve our lives. Be on the lookout for new healthy recipes or routines. Seek out material to expand your mind. Strengthen your sprit with uplifting messages and songs.

In other words, never get comfortable with where you are and let life pass you by. But we all know that it's just not that simple, especially if you may have gotten off to a bad start in life. Challenge yourself every day to be your best possible person and be willing to acknowledge your shortcomings. This is the first step in successfully learning new behaviors.

Finally, always be willing to try something new. You never know... that one new idea, new person, new place, or new thing may be the very thing that helps start your journey to a transformed life and help you live your life in an entirely new way. Here are a few techniques to help you get on the Road to Your Renewal:

- Find a local spa or health club.

- Go to the gym and work out all of the stress that you are experiencing in your life.

- Go to a spa and get a massage on a regular basis.

- Go to a place of worship to get an inspiring and encouraging word.

- Do not try to do this alone.

- Consider getting a coach or a therapist for help.

There are so many places available that you can go to get the help you need these days. You just have to avail yourself to them and let life flow. An anonymous quote says "Nature often holds up a mirror so we can see more clearly the ongoing processes of growth, renewal, and transformation in our lives."

What you have learned in this chapter about the necessity of getting a renewal will help to move you forward on your journey to totally transform your life. Be sure to use this DESTINATION TRANSFORMATION workbook to chart your progress.

NAVIGATE YOUR RENEWAL

As you go through the process of renewal you will be challenged to be honest with yourself and find new ways of being and doing things. Your life can be transformed as you begin to carefully look at where you are right now and determine the direction that your life needs to take.

Honestly answering the following questions about the renewal of your life:

1. What is the one new thing that you can do new this week?

2. How might your thinking be outdated and unable to serve you in your future?

3. What do you think is the basis for this way of thinking?

4. How would you categorize your style or way of doing things now?

5. Are you open or closed minded?

6. Are your current behaviors able to sustain your dreams for tomorrow?

7.   Do you ever find yourself saying, "What's wrong, why can't things stay the way things are?

8.   Is your life telling you that it is time for you to try something new, what is it?

9.   What is your plan to implement that new thing?

10. How soon could you start?

11. How will you measure your progress?

UP NEXT...

Our next turn will be on The Road to your Reinvention...

➤ The Road to Your Reinvention

> *Do what is easy and your life will be hard. Do what is hard and your life will become easy – Les Brown*

As we travel on The Road to Your Reinvention, and I will show you how to transform difficulties into opportunities and totally change your life. You will learn how these life altering situations have profitable potential. On this part of our journey, you will have the opportunity think more deeply about the quality of your life.

Begin by thinking about the last time you saw dramatic change in your life. When was the last time that something so dramatic occurred that it moved you in a completely unexpected direction? What was one thing that brought about the change?

- Was it a diagnosis from a doctor, or a painful divorce or a loss of a job?

- Was it sudden or was a process involved?

- Did you feel angry, sad, anxious?

Sometimes it takes a dramatic experience to get you to wake up. Learning to turn every negative situation into a positive one is the game changer. I will show you how to use a powerful technique that will give you the chance to get a fresh start again and again. This fresh start may be exactly what you need to totally transform your life.

Earlier in this program, you were taught to recognize the need for renewal to live a more fulfilled life. But there are times when renewal is just not enough, and you need to completely reinvent yourself. In other words, renewal works well when you simply need a fresh approach, and you feel that your circumstances are relatively acceptable. You feel comfortable with getting a few tweaks here and there. That's the time that you merely need to take a step back and look at things from another perspective. If we are honest, we would admit that there is always room for improvement.

There comes a time in life when nothing seems to be working, even after you have exhausted all of your resources, and you still see no real change in sight. After you have reviewed your life, rediscovered your dreams, received revelation, and taken advantage of the time to renew, you come to realize that your old paradigms no longer work anymore. This is when you know you need a total overhaul, and you realize that you need to do something radically different...like reinvent yourself.

Your life may be telling you that it's time to shift into a completely new state of existence because what worked in one season will not work in another. For example, just like you wouldn't wear a bathing suit in the wintertime, you should be very careful about what you "wear" in the different seasons of your life.

Let's use the analogy of the butterfly. There comes a time when the caterpillar must change, or it will die. It must go through the process of metamorphosis and the same is true for you. You can get to the point in your life that if you don't do something dramatically different, you risk crushing your hopes and forfeiting your dreams. When you see yourself like the butterfly and intentionally go through the process of metamorphosis that you can be confident that when you emerge from the process, a whole new life can begin. But you must be willing to submit to the process.

In the same way the adult butterfly hardly resembles its earlier caterpillar stage... You too will no longer be crawling but soaring! In order to take on this totally different form, you must be prepared to think differently. You will also be required to act differently to complete a reinvention transformation.

To begin this leg of your journey, the first thing that you need to do is take an inventory to see where you are in the process. Use this technique and begin by honestly answering the following questions:

- How am I doing?

- What am I doing?

- Is it working?

A reinvention requires total commitment to shift your entire course in life in the direction that you want it to go. This could mean that you completely uproot yourself and move to a different place. Or it may just mean that you have to get rid of negative fiends and get around an entirely different group of positive people. Or even do things in a completely different order in your daily routine.

The first critical step to shifting your attitude if you want to reinvent yourself is to receive guidance from someone to whom you can be accountable to help you shift from an attitude that maintains the status quo. Too often we try to handle difficult situations on our own using old methods. This will only result in a cycle of failure. You must realize that different seasons will require different strategies. Having this awareness is what will help make it easier for you to move forward into a totally new way of being.

Going through a reinvention is much like getting an extreme makeover. This is critical to help you change the way you see yourself...

...the way you think about yourself...

...the way you talk to yourself...

...the way you talk about yourself...

...it will even change the way people talk about, think about, and see you too!

Sometimes this level of transformation comes as a result of traumatic circumstances that knocks you off your feet. When your whole world is turned upside down, you can expect that nothing will ever be the same again. If you are honest, you may admit that this level of awakening was needed, or you would never change. Sometimes it takes days, weeks, months and even years before you can figure out what has happened. But to shift out of one dimension of dissatisfaction and defeat into another more gratifying existence, this will require your maximized effort.

It is not what makes you fall that matters, but how you get back up. During these critical times you must be humble enough to get the help you need to be guided in the right direction.

These are the times that you are forced to get help especially after you make an honest assessment of how attached you are to our old life. You must be willing to get help to eliminate whatever stands in the way of your progress. Determining to change old ways of doing things may mean a bit of discomfort. At this point of your reinvention, you have to persevere and press past every obstacle. Be determined to do what it takes and make a dynamic shift. Stop at nothing.

For example, if you have had a health crisis, this is the time to make up your mind that you will do what you have to do to live in perfect health, but you need support to make the change. If you had a job loss, now may be the time to work on your new business idea, you may need a business coach to help you make the shift. If you have seen a broken relationship, this may be the perfect time to get a life coach to help you work on the new and improved you!

The outcome of your reinvention will bring you a new identity. So start by assessing who you are now. Now determine who you really want to be and move toward that with absolute fervor. Get the support you need so you can totally transform your life one day at a time with a less time and effort than if you tried to do it all alone. And when you are done, you will love the person you have become.

What you have learned will help you on your journey for a totally transformed life. Be sure to use this DESTINATION TRANSFORMATION workbook to chart your progress.

NAVIGATE YOUR REINVENTION

In order to go through the process of transformation you must believe that you can experience dynamic change in every area of your life. It will happen if you desire it with all your heart. You must be willing to do what it takes to reinvent yourself so that you can look more like the vision that you have for your life.

Honestly answer the following questions:

1. What are some radical changes do you know needs to happen in your life?

2. What are some radical changes you know you need but have resisted?

3. Why do you think you resisted those changes?

4. What is your strategy for handling the crises that arise in your life?

5. List some things you will do even in the most chaotic of circumstances, to transform your life?

6. What are three dynamic action steps that you will take to bring you closer to fulfilling your dream of a totally transformed life?

UP NEXT...

Our next turn is on to the Road to Your Responsibility.

Navigational Direction 6

The Road to Your Responsibility

> *If you take responsibility for yourself, you will develop a hunger to accomplish your dreams – Les Brown*

Welcome to this sixth session of Destination: TRANSFORMATION eCourse. We are at the halfway mark of this leg of the journey to transform your life. You are making amazing progress. Keep up the great work!

In this session you will begin as you think about the level of opportunities available in your life and determine how well you have handled those opportunities. You will learn a whole new way to approach your responsibilities that will literally transform your life. It's been said by Whitney M. Young, Jr. that "It is better to be prepared for an opportunity and not have one than to have an opportunity and not be prepared."

When we talk about opportunities, the first thing that we realize is that we are presented with many of them. You have numerous opportunities to activate the techniques in this Destination Transformation eCourse. The real question is whether or not you will take the responsibility for what you are learning and implement these tools into in your life. Activation is the only way that we can see real change. The way to take full responsibility when opportunities are presented to you, is to give every opportunity your full attention and absolute best effort. This is easier said than done.

We prove our level of responsibility with our level of performance. It is difficult to give a one hundred percent effort to something that you do not love. But things only begin to change when you take one hundred percent responsibility for your choices, both good and bad. For example, many people work at jobs they hate. You have the option to complain about how much you hate your job. Or you can take advantage of the option to develop yourself and look for another one.

When we open our minds and realize that we always have options, it becomes easier to explore what those options are. When you take responsibility for your life, you make the most of where you are until you can do better. Regardless of that happens in your life, you are responsible for how you will react in every situation. When you accept responsibility for where your life is right now, you are empowered to take control of your life. Then you recognize that only you have the power to change your life. When you accept responsibility for your life, you avoid blaming others for your misfortunes.

For example, you can't blame others for when you do a poor job at work. When you take responsibility, you understand that your work reflects you and is connected to the value you bring to others. You also understand that your work is your signature. You recognize that your work is your opportunity to prosper and transform your life. When you work responsibly, whatever you do, you do it with a sense of service, pride, and excellence. Everything you do and everywhere you go should be positively influenced by your touch. This is what it looks like when you take full responsibility for your actions.

But regardless of how good of an idea it is to be responsible for yourself, there yet exists opposing forces that attempt to get in the way of your progress. Your friends can be jealous about your new house. Your family questions your desire to go to school and improve yourself. Your co-workers are threatened when you go for the promotion. And what they think about you is not your responsibility. Therefore, it is critical to understand that despite your desires, some people, places and things are just out of your control.

But what is in your control is how you react to these types of scenarios and learn the skills to navigate past these obstructive behaviors. Consider the following techniques when faced with opposition that comes from the least expected places:

- Don't participate – Often we give our enemies too much time and attention by giving too much free press when complaining about what someone else did wrong. Advertising is expensive and too often we give it away for free.

- Don't blame others for your problems – Do yourself a favor and take responsibility for the choices you made to get you where you are and better use that energy for strategically planning your success. With a warlike resistance, choose to remain focused on your dreams. Decide to move forward with your plans in spite of negative influences. Refuse to be distracted, unable to make the wise choices needed to secure your goals for the future.

- Don't get out of control - The worst thing you can do is to fall into a trap and get out of control and immediately react. Take responsibility for the outcomes and develop a plan of action to move forward in a positive manner. It is your responsibility to get disoriented and develop strategies on how you will get and stay on top.

- Don't blame yourself - Even worse than blaming others for your problems is blaming yourself. What does not stop us from without, will stop us from within. It has been said that sometimes we can be our own worst enemy. Don't doubt yourself. Don't make excuses for not achieving. This only makes you feel inferior. Don't make excuses for your poor behavior. Excuses only give you permission to settle for less than the best. Never settle for less than what you deserve. Be very careful what you tell yourself. If you say "you can" or you say "you can't", either way, you're right. Don't make excuses and settle where you are.

Don't allow negative thoughts about your personal limitations to get the best of you. Take responsibility and develop your strengths. Determine how you will turn every obstacle into an opportunity. Alexander Graham Bell once said that "When one door closes another opens; but we often look so long and so regretfully upon the closed door that we do not see the one which has opened for us.

On the Road of Your Responsibility, be prepared to go above and beyond anywhere that you have gone before. Be determined to dream your highest dream and take full responsibility for your life and you will be prepared to embark upon the opportunity of a lifetime. When you do this, you will be ready go to an entirely new level of success in your life. Be sure to use this DESTINATION TRANSFORMATION workbook to chart your progress.

NAVIGATE YOUR RESPONSIBILITY

Continue your journey and answer the following questions about how you responsibly handle the opportunities that are presented to you. SMART Goals are: Specific, Measurable, Attainable, Realistic, and Time-Based.

1. What S.M.A.R.T. goals do you want to accomplish in the next 30 days?

2. What is your 3-step action plan to accomplish your goals?

3. When faced with opposition when attempting to fulfill your goals, how do you tend to behave?

4. Write a simple plan on how you will persevere and accomplish your goals even in the midst of opposition.

* Don't let anything get in the way of you accomplishing your goal

* Take personal responsibility and don't make excuses

* Don't blame anyone for your inability to succeed.

* Move forward and do whatever it takes to fulfill your dreams.

UP NEXT...

Up next, let's take the Road to Your Reason

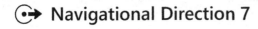

↱ The Road to Your Reason

> *Help others achieve their dreams and you will achieve yours – Les Brown*

Welcome to this seventh session of the Destination: TRANSFORMATION eCourse. In this session you will explore your total reason for being alive. You will also have an opportunity to think more deeply about the purpose behind your dreams, and desires. You will learn how to understand the deep connection between your deepest heart's desire and your reason for being. You will know with all certainty that your purpose for being here is to fulfill the very dream that is in your heart. When you look at your dreams this way, you become more intentional about doing whatever it takes to make your dream a reality because your life depends on it!

Many people flounder about in life because they do not have a purpose, an objective toward which to work. —George Halas, American Football Coach

You must have clear life goals that you are working towards in order for them to be accomplished in your life. There are times when people are unsure of their purpose because they compare themselves to others. But your assignment is not dependent upon what anyone else is doing. It is important not to let anything or what anyone is doing get in the way of you achieving your goals. It is necessary not to let anything or anyone get in the way of you achieving this goal.

Then there are times when you are unsure of you purpose because you are comparing yourself to others. You may feel inferior because there are certain things that they can do that you cannot. It is absolutely critical that you find your own path in life and drive on that road to reach your own personal destiny. Embrace the fact that there are certain things that only you were created to do. You are equipped with your own brand of gifts, talents, and abilities to accomplish what only you were meant to do. When you discover and activate those attributes, you recognize that you are a gift to the world. But you have to be willing to do the work necessary to mine out the purpose deep within your heart so that you can ultimately fulfill your purpose for being alive.

Oftentimes I hear people say, "I just don't know what *I* am supposed to do!" As a result, uncertainty has plagued every area of their lives, leaving a very painful void. This constant ambiguity breeds a life of insecurity and a total lack of self-confidence. This is the reason why so many people fall prey to addictive and even abusive behaviors. When people are dissatisfied with the way things are, they seek to become disconnected from their present reality in search of relief from the pain of dissatisfaction.

If you are going to transform your life, you must decide to discover your reason for being alive. When you are not intentional about fulfilling your purpose, you leave the outcomes of your life to chance. But leaving everything up to fate could be fatal. Even more dangerous than comparing yourself to others is to put your destiny in the hands of others. If you are going to achieve your purpose, it is critical that you become empowered to realize your own dreams.

You must make a decision to live out your full potential. Only you have the power to do this. When you are confident about your reason for being on this earth, then you feel more compelled to fulfill your purpose. When you are aware of the power that lies within you, you move your life towards you, fulfilling your destiny.

You have to also understand that discovering your purpose is a process. This process is pregnant with potential. It's a lot like the developmental process of natural pregnancy. For example, when you first get pregnant, no one can really tell. You may even decide to keep it a secret for a while.

Likewise, it is much the same when you are pregnant with purpose. Once your purpose is initially revealed to you, you may not want to reveal it to anyone right away. Because you are just getting used to the idea yourself, you may want to incubate and nurture this precious seed for a season. You do this because you may not feel comfortable sharing with people who do not understand the transformation that is about to take place in your life.

Likewise, you should be careful with whom you share your dreams. Beware of those who will not understand what you are trying to do and seek to abort your vision. When you are pregnant with purpose, you are keenly aware of the changes that take place during this distinctive process. But regardless of how much you may want to keep it to yourself, eventually, your purpose will begin to show.

Just like any normal pregnancy, after you conceive, when you nurture and protect your seed, the dream will grow. You will eventually have to communicate your purpose through your words, your actions and your attitude. Those closest to you will notice that there is something different about you. They may not be able to put their finger on it, but they will see a change, nonetheless. But you still may not feel ready to share the news with the world quite yet.

That's okay because after all, it's your prerogative, and it's your dream! When you feel it's the right time to share your purpose, be sure to connect with the right people who understand the direction that you are going in. You should never try to fulfill your destiny alone. You will know who these people are because they will help support you on your journey toward fulfilling your purpose. They will play an important role as they act as midwives that affirm you every step of the way in the fulfillment of your purpose. Their support is immeasurable, so choose wisely.

When you go through the birthing process of your purpose, you will go through many phases, and unexpected changes. During the natural birthing process, you will go through many transitions and changes. Similar to that of a natural birth, purpose has seasons in which to evolve and unfold. We can break it down into trimesters.

THE FIRST TRIMESTER

During the first trimester of birthing your purpose, you begin to conceive the idea in your mind that your life has more meaning. Once you begin to get this sense deep within your heart, you will know that this is your time to fulfill it.

THE SECOND TRIMESTER

When your purpose begins to show, you must be prepared to deliver the purpose that you embody. As you prepare, you begin to feel more confident in your power to create a beautiful life for yourself and bless everyone around you.

THIRD TRIMESTER

Now is the time to prepare to deliver. You must be willing to do whatever it takes to ready yourself for the birthing position. This might mean that you go back to school, or even take courses like this one, to keep you focused and moving forward on your journey to a totally transformed life. In a natural birth you can take Lamaze classes to learn how to breathe during your delivery. Likewise, it will take courage and perseverance. You will need to learn how to take deep breaths of courage as you press your way into your purpose. Do everything in your power to make your delivery a smooth one. Stop at nothing until you fulfill your purpose and reason for being alive!

Here's a technique that you can use to discover your purpose in life and your reason for being alive:

- Start by making a list of all of the things that you are passionate about and list the things that really concern you about your life, your work, your community, your world. Recognize the possibility that these are the things that you were created to address. You will never feel fulfilled until you deal with these things in some positive way. You will not be satisfied until you contribute to solving the problem.

- It's okay to start small. Just get started and your reason for being will begin to quickly unfold. Pick one issue and start to develop an action plan on how you can make an impact. You will suddenly realize that your reason for being brings more meaning and satisfaction into your life.

Helen Keller said "Many people have a wrong idea of what constitutes true happiness. It is not attained through self-gratification, but through fidelity to a worthy purpose." What you have learned in this chapter will help to move you forward on your journey to totally transform your life of purpose. Be sure to use this DESTINATION TRANSFORMATION workbook to chart your progress.

NAVIGATE YOUR REASON

Your life can be literally transformed as you begin to get a better understanding about what your purpose is for being in the world.

Think honestly about what you believe to be your purpose in life as you continue your journey and answer the following questions:

1. In what ways can you cultivate these transformational messages that help to bring you closer to your life purpose?

2. What are some things that you can do to get past the obstacles that try to keep you from fulfilling your purpose?

3. What are some of the ways you can activate your newfound realities?

4. List one way that you will celebrate the discovery of your purpose for being alive.

UP NEXT...

Our next turn is onto the Road to Your Relationships.

The Road To Your Relationships

> *Don't let someone else's opinion of you*
> *become your reality – Les Brown*

Welcome to this 8th session of Destination: TRANSFORMATION eCourse. As we travel together, you will discover how to make some electric connections! During this session you will have the opportunity to think more critically about your current connections and have the chance to assess all of the associations in your life.

As you take the time to make this assessment, you will be able to determine whether each relationship is an asset, or a liability. If you are honest and determine if your important relationships add to you or subtract from you, you will be amazed at the results.

Could you imagine what life would be like if you had mutually beneficial, loving, caring relationships in your life? Many people only dream of finding the right person that could support them on their journey to fulfill your dreams. It is vital for you understand how important it is to be more discerning about the company you keep. Your future depends on it.

You can learn how to literally attract the right people into your life by being intentional and choose the people who have the capacity to support you on your journey toward fulfilling your dreams. You will learn how to be ready for these people to come into your life.

Many times, when people think about relationships, they think about dating and marriage. That's because these are more than casual relationships and should not be taken lightly. They can make you or break you! In order for you to see a total life transformation, you must also never underestimate the importance of all your relationships. This includes your business connections and colleagues. The right friendships can also make an indelible impact on your future. Lois Wyse said "A good friend is a connection to life—a tie to the past, a road to the future, the key to sanity in a totally insane world."

The people you choose to interact with will have a direct impact on your success in life. It's the people that you spend the most time with that will determine your outcomes in life. You should never take any of these connections lightly. It is critical to your future that you make the best possible relationships choices.

All too often, we take this fact for granted. We casually choose the people who will share our lives. We expect that they will support us in the fulfillment of our dreams. But this is not always the case. This is why we must be intentional in choosing people that we believe will respect our potential and support the direction that we are headed.

In other words, on the Road to Your Relationships, use the technique of choosing all your companions with your future in mind. This will mean developing the skills necessary to make the right choices by setting the criteria well in advance.

Make a list of the qualities that you want to see in the people that you bring into your life. It doesn't matter how long or short the list is. All that matters is that you are honest and thorough as you possibly can. Then, begin to look for these qualities in the people that you associate with. If the qualities that you long for are in these people, they are keepers!

If not, you need to renegotiate the relationship and not allow those people into your inner circle. Too many people make the assumption that their friends or mate will support them through difficult times or even when they develop personally or professionally. But based upon the high divorce rates, we can see that although two people may have become married, they may not necessarily be on the same page. Although two people connect and choose to be married, they could be moving in two distinctly different directions. This may not be all bad if they have the foresight to come to an understanding about the structure of their relationship in advance.

Each partner must be open and willing to accept their mate even when they make positive changes in the future. This is the foundation for a loving, lasting relationship. But this is not always the case. This is why so many marriages are unsuccessful and over half of them end in divorce. One reason is that two people merely enter into an arrangement or contractual agreement.

A contract is an agreement that can be ended by either party at any time for any reason. Many times, people get married thinking that they have entered into a covenant but come equipped with a back-up plan just in case things don't work out. It is important to understand the difference between a contract and a covenant. A covenant is a commitment you make a until death. This is what most marriages should embody.

If either partner comes to the table with an alternate plan already in mind, there is clearly no intention of participating in a committed covenant. Relationships fail because there is no real clarity about the level of expectations. This kind of relationship may not foster an environment for growth and development. At the first sign that something undesirable takes place, the contractual agreement is placed in jeopardy and more often than not, somebody pays dearly. The focus is primarily upon present needs, wants, and conditions. When one of the partners is self-centered, all further interactions threaten to end the relationship because only one person is benefitting. This is a formula for disaster.

Marriage is not just about marrying the right person, it's also about *being* the right person. You should always focus on how you can be your best possible person first. You should give your best effort to be what you want to see. You should do this rather than wondering whether or not you have found the right person to spend your life with. If we focus on being the right person, this investment will dynamically change the quality of your life as an individual as well as the relationship. When you focus on being your best, you increase the likelihood of having a great relationship and there is no need to search for better options.

This is true of friendships and business relationships as well. We need to know with some level of confidence that the person we have chosen will be there for us when we need them the most. Sometimes we unknowingly pattern ourselves after the dysfunctional relationship models that we experienced in our nuclear family that we grew up in. Subconsciously we believe that these familiar patterns are normal.

This is why it is easy to follow suit and produce more of the same dysfunction, if not worse. One of the biggest problems with locating good relationships is when people carry baggage from the past. You need to be honest and take the time you need to heal from previous hurts. You need to de-bag from the issues you have encountered from previously unsuccessful relationships because if you are not careful, you will transfer old issues onto a new promising relationship. When you do this, you subconsciously sabotage your own success because you always expect the worst and history will conveniently continue to repeat itself. It is imperative to give yourself time to heal from past hurts so that you can have the capacity to see any new experience clearly without the shadow of past pain.

If you have ever found yourself asking, "Why does this keep happening to me?" it's probably a good time to stop and reflect on how your own behaviors are actually creating the negative cycle of undesired outcomes. When you take responsibility for your choices, then make the adjustments necessary, you increase the possibilities for better outcomes in the future. It may be helpful to seek the professional assistance of a psychologist or minister for help to avoid subconsciously repeating vicious cycles. Studying courses like this one will help you open up new possibilities and enhance your relationship skills.

When you raise your awareness to your own shortcomings, you are more forgiving of others. When you accept the fact that you are not perfect, you will not put unrealistic demands on others. This positions you for the right people to come into your life because you are ready to see them through your new lens of acceptance.

If you ever find yourself having to say to someone you love, "I thought you knew how much I love you," you are probably not putting enough into your relationship's emotional bank account to sustain a rich, loving, lasting relationship. In order to get what you want in the relationship, you must learn to make continuous deposits so you can make the necessary withdrawals when you need them the most. Don't make the habitual mistake of having an overdrawn emotional bank account.

In the banking industry, this it is considered abusive neglect and warrants closing the account. If your relationship emotional bank account is consistently overdrawn, you will eventually see its closure. Be intentional and learn how to consistently give and take. Pay close attention to your partner's needs so you will not be taken by a surprise ending. Develop your skills and get the tools you need to intentionally nurture your relationship. Destiny is about the decisions that we make to live your absolute best life. When you are intentional, you are selective with those who will share your journey of a lifetime. Part of those decisions include who we choose to share our life with. Choose to make some electric connections by thinking critically about your current connections and have the chance to assess all of the associations in your life. Jack Kornfield said "When we get too caught up in the busyness of the world, we lose connection with one another—and ourselves." Determine the value of each relationship and be you will be astounded the outcomes.

Be sure to use this DESTINATION TRANSFORMATION workbook to chart your progress.

NAVIGATE YOUR RELATIONSHIPS

It has been said that you are only as good as the company you keep. You may want to have this portion of this transformational dialog with a significant other or close friend and answer the following questions honestly:

1. How healthy would you say your relationships are right now?

2. Do you feel nurtured and safe enough to share your truth?

3. How you feel when people support you?

4. How about when they do not?

5. If you are in relationship with people that you do not feel safe around...

    a) Why don't you feel safe?

    b) Why are you still around them?

6. What are the types of people that you need to bring into or remove from your life?

7. Are you connected with people who support the things that you want to do?

8. How are the people with whom you associate encouraging you to fulfill your destiny dreams?

9. How can you surround yourself with genuinely caring people to support the vision and mission for your life?

UP NEXT...

Up next, The Road to Your Results

↱ **The Road to Your Results**

> *As you reach your goals set new ones. That is how you grow and become a more powerful person. - Les Brown*

Welcome to this 9th session of Destination: TRANSFORMATION eCourse.

In this session, you will learn techniques on how to get exactly the results that you are looking for in your life. You will also discover how to get better outcomes in the circumstances that you find yourself. I will share with you how to better prepare for your future so that you can get the results that you want for the long haul. Abraham Lincoln said that "The best thing about the future is that it only comes one day at a time."

To begin your journey together, ask yourself a few questions:

• What is it that you would like to see happen in the very near future?

• What conditions are needed to manifest your future success and best life ever?

- What steps do you need to take to manifest this success in your life?

- Can you visualize future success?

- Exactly what do you want to see?

Sometimes, you cannot successfully get the results that you are looking for because you are stuck in the past. This happens when you've experienced a series of bad circumstances. When this happens, you make a subconscious determination that this is the way things will always be. When you do this, you give up the fight to have a better future and surrender to your current circumstances believing that things will never change regardless of how bad they may be.

As a result of vicious cycles, eventually your outlook becomes pessimistic, downward spiral and you wonder if there will ever be anything to look forward to. When you take on this mindset, life becomes even more pitiful as you experience one setback after another.

Napoleon Hill, in *Think and Grow* Rich said that "There is very little difference in people. But that little difference makes a big difference. The little difference is attitude. The big difference is whether it's a positive or negative attitude." It is critical to understand that your attitude determines the level of your altitude in life. You must remain positive about your present and reduce the negative feelings of anxiety over what has already happened in the past. You cannot change the past. But you can learn from it to positively impact the future. In order to obtain to the promise of your dreams you must learn to adjust your attitude. Then you must be intentional about overcoming the difficulties of your past. This is accomplished as you redirect your thinking in a way that does not allow your past to contaminate your present.

What you can do is learn how to extrapolate the messages from the mess that you have experienced and discard anything that will not serve you in your future. There are some valuable lessons that can be salvaged from the wreckage. But this can be difficult to do because you have a memory that continues to play scenes from the past. This type of thinking gives the illusion of an eternal drama that has no end.

But although these may be a continuum, you have to be able to separate your past from your present and your present from your future. When you further explore this idea of the past, present, and future, you can make the connection between the three components of who you are. —Body, soul, and spirit.

Understanding this concept has a direct impact on how you see yourself. It is no surprise that your mind holds your memories; but it might interest you to know that your body also has a memory. This is easily understood when you have experienced physical trauma. Your mind can go back to a time when it experienced the trauma. Then your mind can trigger your body, which remembers the trauma and physically constricts muscles, organs, and tissues identical to the first incident. This experience can cause a substantial amount of pain.

Keeping this in mind, it is vitally important that you learn how to resolve negative thoughts and memories as quickly as possible. This is the first step to breaking the vicious cycles that keeps you in an unhealthy emotional state. It is this emotional imbalance that will keep you from being able to think clearly about our future. You must be intentional to be free from the stresses of the past if you want to get the results that you desire in the present.

Take a moment and determine how many of your own choices led you to where you are right now. You must make up in your mind to leave the past in the past. I heard it said that when the past calls you, don't answer, because it has nothing new to tell you! Furthermore, the past cannot be changed. Although it may be important for historical purposes, it is not entirely reliable for future predictions regarding your life. It would be in your best interest to activate the closure of any unresolved matters as quickly as possible and move on. Your focus should be on the promise of a new day. Your energy would be used in being directed towards what it will take to get the result that you desire in life.

Whether you realize it or not, you have the power to change the outcomes in your life. Your thoughts are like seeds that, when planted, grow into the fruits of your life. In this way, you are what you think about. If you have a great life, it will be mostly because you have a great thought life. The opposite is also true; if you have a great deal of negativity around you, it is probably as a result of the seeds of negativity that you sowed in a past season. Now you are reaping the fullness of what you planted which consequently ended with a negative harvest. The good news is that you can plant better seeds for a better crop next time around.

You should become keenly aware of what has prevented a good harvest in your life and be willing to address the source of the problem. When you learn from the mistakes of your past then you will be informed about what to do to reap a better harvest in the future.

Here is a technique that you can use If you want to see more positive results in your life:

Embrace the idea of the need for improvement in every area of your life. As Peter McWilliams *said, You cannot afford the luxury of one negative thought!* Train yourself to be more aware of these negative thought patterns and behaviors...Then seek to completely eradicate them from your life by doing the following:

- Intentionally maintain high levels of possibility in any given situation. Always see the possibilities, regardless of the circumstances. As you pay close attention to your thoughts and behaviors, you can be more intentional about arresting thoughts intended to sabotage your future. Refuse to allow your current circumstances to limit the outcomes of your entire future.

- When you find yourself dissatisfied with life, take a moment and acknowledge that your current situation is only temporary. Although there may be circumstances that are beyond your control, you are not as powerless as you would like to believe. You do have the ability to positively influence the outcome of your life. It's all a matter of how you approach the things of your past and the things in your present that will ultimately affect the things of your future.

I have discovered that regardless of how bad the conditions, I can determine how depressed, despondent, and diseased that I will be. When you honestly assess the status of your life, you will discover that you can use your decision-making power and choose to change.

Once you do this, you will be empowered and no longer fall victim to your circumstances or the actions of others. Blaming others is a waste of time and robs you of too much precious time and energy. Embrace the fact that you made a decision to allow their actions to negatively affect your life. Now, learn from that and make another powerful decision to begin the process to disallow anyone that kind of access. This technique will help you begin to create healthy boundaries to protect your well-being.

You will also need to develop an action plan and strategies that bring your life into alignment with your vision for your life. Develop disciplines that will sustain you in the difficult times. When you are disciplined in this way, your life becomes consistently stable. You will no longer be swayed by every circumstance that confronts your life.

Another technique is to create disciplines, such as consistently spending quality time in prayer or meditation, listening to inspirational messages, reading positive material, a healthy diet and exercise. These are great places to start if you are determined to see the results of a transformed life.

Implementing these techniques will help you to get better outcomes that you are looking for in your life. This will help you to better prepare for your future so that you can get the results that you want to see in your lifetime. What you have learned in this chapter will move you forward on your journey to totally transform your life. Be sure to use this DESTINATION TRANSFORMATION workbook to chart your progress.

NAVIGATE YOUR RESULTS

Think about how your past impacts your future and answer honestly the following questions:

1. What are some things from your past that are preventing you from enjoying the present?

2. What are some things that are happening in the present that threaten to rob the success of your future?

3. What is the one thing that you could do to ensure that you have a better quality of life right now?

4. What action steps could you take now that your future self will thank you for?

5. What would that success look like? feel like? Smell like? Sound like?

6. Why do you feel that it is important for you to do these things?

7.   When will you start?

8.   When can you anticipate completion?

UP NEXT...

Our next turn is onto the Road to Your Reflections.

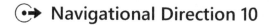

↱ The Road to Your Reflection

> *No matter how bad it is or how bad it gets*
> *I am going to make it. – Les Brown*

Welcome to this 10th session of Destination: TRANSFORMATION eCourse. In this session, you will discover how to transform your life by simply changing your mind and learn some powerful techniques on how to think in a way that exceeds your every expectation. As you activate these techniques, your life will increasingly change for the better. John F. Kennedy once shared that "Change is the law of life. And those who look only to the past or present are certain to miss the future."

Take a minute and think about the things that you are looking forward to accomplishing in your life. Think about the probability of these things actually happening.

* How confident do you feel about this probability?

* What are some of the things that makes you think it will happen?

- What are some things that makes you believe that it may not happen?

Life is filled with expectations, both good and bad. If you can learn how to shift your expectations to be more of what you want to see, the difference in the outcomes you see is nothing short of remarkable. If you can believe it, you will begin to see an amazing turnaround in your life.

It is not unusual for people to have expectations about their future. But you can raise your level of expectation so that it will be more likely that you will get what you would like to see. It is what you think about that can make you or break you. If you are going to achieve anything notable in your life, you must realize that what you reflect on will have a tremendous impact upon the outcomes for your life. As Les Brown says, "What you think about, you bring about."

When you have a healthy mental attitude, you have the powerful opportunity to attract good things into your life and raise the likelihood of your dreams coming to pass. A good mental attitude about what you expect to see will build your confidence. As you focus on the possibilities in your life, you become more motivated. Your rate of frustration lowers because you have a clearer sense of direction. Frustration is always a sign that there are conflicting visions going on in your mind, and the one you want is not winning. It is also a sign that you are moving in the wrong direction because life should be a flow.

When you understand that you are identified by your expectations, you will quickly begin to organize your life around the most positive ones. When you make this your top priority, this increases the probability of the things that you desire coming to pass. When your thoughts are more positively defined, your potential is enhanced. When you consistently activate this technique in your life, you are consistently breathing new energy into the things you expect to see.

In order to gain this new sense of fulfillment, clearly communicate your expectations with regularity wherever you go. When you have a clear set of expectations, you are more likely to attract others who are willing to help you to accomplish your goals. Then the entire universe will collectively collaborate with you to bring your dreams to reality. Your confident expectations will creatively inform the world of their existence and that they are ready to materialize. But this will require faith.

Faith sees the impossible. Faith sees what does not already exist. Faith sees what can happen. Faith matures into trust and is founded upon a strong level expectation. Fear is the enemy of faith and must be conquered before you can enter this level of expectation. It is in this dimension of expectation that faith can be reproduced and multiplied.

This is why it is so important to be around faith-filled people. Faith is increased when it is comingled with the faith of others. But the same is also true when you associate with people who live in fear. Your fear and their fear will reproduce exponentially and reinforce more fear. This is why it is critical to associate yourself with people of faith as you advance toward the fulfillment of our dreams.

Having expectation is a lot like having a baby in the womb of our thoughts. During this kind of pregnancy there are things that are expected like physical changes, growth, and a change in food cravings. Then there is stretching, pressure, weight changes, and so on. As with a natural birth, there is also the unexpected, like a sudden kick or a sudden growth spurt. But regardless of the challenges, the mother is inspired to persevere because she knows that soon a beautiful baby will be born.

Like an expectant mother, you too must persevere through the momentary discomforts in life because you know that something beautiful is about to be born into your life. What you think about has the powerful potential to materialize. When you realize that you become what you think about, you will be more careful and selective with what you allow to enter and entertain in your mind. You would also not think so casually about the images that come across our televisions, computers and other forms of media that you are bombarded with every day.

Some things that you allow to casually enter your mind are not as harmless as you would like to believe. It is critical to be very cautious about the intrusion of these images into your space and safeguard against their negative effects. As a practice, when an unsuspecting, harmful image comes into your mind, just like with a computer virus, be intentional to quickly delete it, disarm it, or destroy it. Proactively render all negative thoughts powerless and ineffective against the well-being of your psyche.

People who have a history of abuse have an imprint of bad memories on their mind. This is the reason they often have dismal outlooks and see no hope for their future. Negative images they see in their daily lives, films, and the media only reinforce this pessimistic orientation.

But Peter McWilliams reminds us that *"You can't afford the luxury of one negative thought.*

You have command of your mind that can be refocused on new perspectives and flooded with positive images and stories. It is possible to shift out of a vicious cycle of negativity and fight to maintain a consistently positive attitude. You can learn how to do this and use the technique of reenactment. This is different from recreation of memories from the past. This is an intentional strategy to make things right in your life.

Try this "Reenactment" technique:

Simply reenact any negative situations that you have experienced and *add* your desired ending. It's like getting a do over! If you forgot the birthday of someone who is important to you... Celebrate it anyway! Don't waste precious time dwelling on your mistakes. Use the energy to make the experience even better. The person will eventually thank you for your sincerity. If they are not thankful then this is probably a relationship that you need to renegotiate, because they are not willing to forgive your faults and failures. Another tip is to not take life so seriously! In addition, don't allow others to make you feel badly about yourself. Your life will begin to move in more positive pathways when you incorporate this technique into your life.

Gratitude is another important technique that helps you to receive the best life has to offer. When you appreciate even the little things, you set yourself up for more good to come into your life. Be naturally thankful for what you have, where you are, and how far you have come in life. You will suddenly notice that you are no longer dwelling on what is not happening, and your total focus is on what IS!

Similarly, when you are ungrateful and discontent, life seems to just spiral downhill. But you can adjust your thoughts and expectations to be thankful for even the smallest things like air, water, food, shelter. See those things as life's true abundance. This type of thinking gives you the latitude to dream bigger than you have ever dreamed before. In order for this to happen you must possess a thought life that facilitates what you want to manifest. The more you do this, you will increase your capacity to see more than you ever imagined. You increase the likelihood of your dreams coming to pass.

When you travel the Road to Your Reflections, it is absolutely vital that you expect the best in order to see the best. You must think the best in order to be your best. When you are your best, you receive the best. You experience the best. Richard M. DeVos lets us know that life...it tends to respond to our outlook, to shape itself to meet our expectations.

As you enter the dimension of a positive expectation, allow your-self to reflect on the best of everything for your life. And what you think about, soon, you will eventually become! Watch your thoughts and change your life!

In this session, you will discover how to transform your life by simply changing your mind and learn some powerful techniques on how to think in a way that exceeds your every expectation. As you activate these techniques, your life will increasingly change for the better.

Ralph Marston says "Don't lower your expectations to meet your performance. Raise your level of performance to meet your expec-tations. Expect the best of yourself, and then do what is necessary to make it a reality. What you have learned will move you forward on your journey to total transformation in your life a reality. If you need additional help with these techniques, be sure to contact me for other powerful resources at DRLAVERNEADAMS.COM.

I care about you, and I want you help you to go further than you ever have before. I am here for you so let's continue our journey together.

NAVIGATE YOUR REFLECTIONS

Your life will be transformed as you get a better understanding regarding the power of your thought life. Honestly answer the following questions:

1.   How do you think your life looks right now?

2.   What is "one thing" that you are hoping to see happen in your life?

3.   Why do you want to see this?

4.   How and when do you think that this "one thing" will happen?

5.   What is the picture in your mind concerning this "one thing"?

6. Now that you have painted a clearer picture for your mind, it can work on bringing it to pass.

*   Focus on the manifestation of this one thing every day in a positive way for the next 30 days. Mark it on your calendar.

*   Pretty soon you will be painting another picture because that one would have already been realized.

UP NEXT...

Our next turn is onto the Road to Your Revolution.

↱ The Road to Your Revolution

> *The easiest thing I ever did was earn a million dollars.*
> *The hardest thing I ever did, and it took years, was believing*
> *I was capable of earning a million dollars. – Les Brown*

Welcome to this 11th session of the Destination: TRANSFORMATION eCourse. In this session you will learn how to revolutionize literally your life as I show you some powerful techniques to recognize the miraculous. Miracles are happening all around you. You may not notice them, but they are there waiting to be accessed. You will learn how you can consistently have miraculous experiences every day. These breathtaking experiences will leave you in awe and wonder. Albert Einstein once said that "There are two ways to live: you can live as if nothing is a miracle; you can live as if everything is a miracle." And, if you are honest, you would admit that there was at least one time that God did something in your life that you knew was impossible for you to do in your own power. You may recall something that you experienced that was out of the ordinary and defied all natural laws.

I am sure that you have heard countless stories of people who escaped impending danger unharmed, without explanation. These people knew that they had lost power over the situation and could in no way control the outcomes. They knew that only a power greater than themselves could have afforded them such a special opportunity to come out alive. It was clear that the radical shift that they experienced drastically revolutionized how they lived their lives.

These people are not only grateful but live the rest of their lives in completely different ways. They know without a shadow of a doubt that the only reason why they are still alive is because of a miracle. As you go through this session, you will learn that these kinds of miraculous experiences will cause you to think radically differently. This will transform the way you live because your awareness will be raised to see more of what is possible. This awareness will deeply change your outcomes and behaviors.

What you will learn will help you become increasingly aware of where and when the miraculous is happening...and that a great deal of things that are happening around you are beyond your control. When you tap into this higher dimension, you begin to hear the symphony of the orchestration of people, places and events that are miraculously moving on your behalf. You will be able to be more keenly aware that all of this was already taking place all around you. You will literally be able to watch as the vehicles of your destiny position you where you are supposed to be, and exactly when you are supposed to be there. And you will begin to see the synchronicity that envelops your entire life and that moves you effortlessly into your purpose.

When you think of the miraculous, you primarily should accept that there is a power greater than yourself orchestrating circumstances that are beyond your control. But what you may not realize is that you can also be an active participant with the miracles that are happening around you! The first thing that you have to do is embrace their existence and acknowledge that they are real.

But the key is for you to look for their manifestation in even the smallest ways.

When you learn how to identify miracles when they happen, you are careful not to ascribe these powerful acts to coincidence. You acknowledge and recognize their manifestation. This is when you come to the realization that God is continuously at work in your life; you simply need to participate with the process. Soon you begin to anticipate that God will move in your situation in an unexpected way and then suddenly, everything begins to change!

This becomes especially important when crisis hits. It may be in your health, your relationships, or your finances. When this happens, you might tend to go into survival mode. But there is another dimension into which you can shift: A miracle mode!

When you open yourself up to the miraculous, you gain a sense of peace and calm regardless of what you might be going through. It is this newfound trust that will literally revolutionize your life. You will no longer walk around in worry or fear. You will have an assurance that your things will work out for your benefit in the end. In this miracle mode you are completely reliant on the power of God. Once this happens, you will never look at crisis the same. You begin to trust that even the most horrific things are going work out in your favor.

Have you ever considered that some of the circumstances that arise in your life have come to strengthen you and your faith? Can you embrace the idea that God wants to get you to a place where you can believe that anything is possible? Sometimes you can only get there one painstakingly step at a time. These steps will force you to move past a faith crisis and move on to what you believe to be true.

Whenever the unexpected or something out of the ordinary occurs, you could be shaken to the core. But when you are grounded on the foundation of faith in the miraculous to assist you, you respond completely differently to these shaky situations.

Then there are times when it's hard to see a good future because you fear the unknown. When you are in this place emotionally, you may get disoriented. You are at a loss to take strategic action to move your life forward because you are confused. There is the temptation is to continue doing what you have been accustomed to doing and to shift into the fear gear. But you must immediately resist this temptation & believe that a miracle is about to happen and that something good will come out of every situation.

Sometimes this is hard because we cannot control the outcomes of the miraculous. But when you begin to embrace the realm of the miraculous, it is no longer possible to stay where you have been. Something has changed, and you can't undo it! You begin to accept the fact that perhaps God has allowed these radical acts for a purpose soon to be revealed. Then you begin to realize that these difficult moments allow you to press your way into a higher dimension. The best think you could do is to surrender. Don't fight it. These things are there for your good.

There are times when you need something cataclysmic to help shift your faith and cause you to do something radically different to transform your life. You will never be the same because these miraculous experiences cause you to believe like never before that all things are possible. That's when you know that these things are happening to align you closer to your destiny.

Helen Keller once said that "When we do the best we can, we never know what miracle is wrought in our life or in the life of another." These kinds of experiences take you to new levels of faith. This is the kind of faith that believes the impossible, feels the intangible, and sees the invisible. This kind of faith can over-come any obstacle and dramatically changes your vision for your life. This is the kind of faith that recognizes miracles happening all around you literally revolutionize your life forever!

NAVIGATE YOUR REVOLUTION

Think honestly about how your feelings about miracles and answer these questions:

1. What is your definition of a miracle?

2. Have you ever witnessed a miracle?

3. Is this something that you can do yourself or is it something that only a power greater than you can perform?

4. Where do you need a miracle to be performed in your life?

5. What will it look like when your miracle happens? Will you recognize it?

6. Are you ready for the miraculous to happen every day of your life?

7. What are you doing to prepare yourself for the miraculous to completely revolutionize your life?

UP NEXT...

Up next, the Road to Your Reward.

 **Life Coaching Lesson 12**

⮡ The Road to Your Reward

> *You will win if you don't quit. Les Brown*

Welcome to this 12th and final session of the Destination: TRANSFORMATION – Your Navigational Roadmap to a Totally Fulfilling, Pretty Amazing, Completely Rewarding Dream Life!

• We have traveled a great deal of territory together. You made a lot of turns to get here, but I hope the journey has revealed some amazing truths about you.

You have learned a great deal of techniques to successfully navigate the road that leads to a rewarding and satisfying life. You understand now how to be more intentional, to identify the things that happened in your past that kept you from advancing and moving forward:

• You have learned how to get on the Road to Review Your Life to better understand where you are and how you got there so that you can know where you are going.

- You have learned how to reignite your sense of wonder as you traveled the Road to Your Rediscovery.

- You have learned how to receive important destiny clues from trusted people who can speak into your life as you traveled the Road to your Revelation.

- You now have techniques that you can use to renew and even reinvent your life as you try new things, go new places and meet new people on the Road to Your Renewal and turned onto the Road to Your Reinvention.

- You know how to maximize every moment as you travel the Road to Your Responsibility.

- You know how to find and fulfill your purpose in life as you travel the Road to Your Reason for being alive.

- You know how to attract some really great people into your life as you travel down the Road to Your Relationships.

- You learned how to adjust your attitude to get the results that you want to see on the Road to Your Results.

- You understand how to guard your thoughts on the Road to Your Reflections.

- And you understand the power of miracles on the Road to Your Revolution.

What could be more rewarding than to use all of these techniques to find that you now have a totally transformed life?

The best thing that you could ever do to have a transformed life is to make one very important decision... That decision is to do whatever it takes to get the life that you want to see and to stop at nothing. You have a very important destiny! Be willing to do whatever it takes to fulfill it! And this fulfillment is your ultimate reward.

This one decision will have a direct impact upon how you live out the rest of your life. This session will help you envision and embrace your very unique future. You will learn how to persevere until your life looks like the destiny dream in your heart.

So, what is the one thing in your life that makes you more aware that you have a very real and unique future? What course of events make it clear that you must take a special direction for your life? As you align yourself with this reality, you become driven by the powerful vision of your dreams. After you are truly exposed to it, nothing can stop you.

If we are to truly fulfill your dreams, and live the rewarding life you desire, your only hope is to cooperate with God, who divinely designed it. This understanding will help you redefine your choices and decisions and set you on your unique destiny path. This is especially important when you feel like things are not happening quite the way you want. This is also important if things are not happening quite as fast as you would like them to.

One thing that you should be clear about in this age of convenience is that the unfolding of destiny is never instantaneous. The process it takes to for destiny to be fulfilled will not be rushed. You will never be able to dash into your destiny. You will not be able to get destiny on demand. If you want to arrive at your destiny destination safely, you must understand the necessity of preparing for it.

There are those who want to go through streamlined processes and then desire to be considered experts. But there are no shortcuts to destiny. Accelerated processes will never give you what only a lifetime of experiences can teach you. What you should ultimately crave are the tools necessary to make an authentic, long-lasting, positive impact on the world regardless of what you are going through in your life.

Some of those tools are the techniques that you learned in this course to live a totally transformed life. And it is only when you are transformed, that you can help others to be transformed. We can only give away the things that we truly possess ourselves. Understand that every object in your life is strategically placed with purpose. Then you can have assurance that everything will work in your favor.

Embrace the fact that every detail of your life is created as part of a larger pattern whose final graphic presentation is nothing short of astounding. And when we come to the realization that we are God's divine project that we can appreciate every motif and flourish that brings depth into our lives. Know with all certainty that from the time that you were conceived in the mind of God, God already imagined your life would be a complete success, because you were created in God's image. You were imprinted with God's destiny dream from the time that you were born. When you fully embrace the masterpiece of your life, you want to become more aligned with the dream that God dreams for your life.

God will go to great lengths to make things possible for you to live a meaningful and rewarding life. Make the necessary decision to follow your dreams regardless of how impossible it seems. Knowing that you have a purpose should be enough to help you to overcome every obstacle and achieve your goals.

Because your destiny is founded in God, the Master Architect, you need to check with the Creator for the instructions on how best to function in it. And because you are a God idea, all things work together according to God's divine purposes in your life when you surrender to God's plan. God has artistically fashioned a fabulous schematic for your life. Once you surrender your life to God, then and only then can you perceive the highly detailed design that belongs to you. This knowledge should inspire you and give you the strength to scale any mountain, cross any river, or leap over any gulf to reach your goal. You should be prepared to participate with God and do whatever it takes to make happen what is already considered a reality in the mind of God. Know that whatever God imagines has the ability to powerfully materialize.

But, in order to obtain this glorious future, you must be prepared to strategically realign, reinvent, and re-create your life to look more like the destiny dream God has for you. There may be times that you will get weary, and your journey may even seem strange to you. I once received a card with a caption that read: "Others can, you cannot! W.B. Howard"

When I first read this, I became angry because I did not understand why I was seemingly being singled out. There may be times that you do not understand why you have to do certain things differently from everyone else. Then I learned that because I had a special purpose, I had to follow the individual path that God had uniquely laid out for my life. You should never try to force your way into your destiny by your own power. You merely need to flow with your destiny and trust that God will bring it to pass.

There are many dimensions that you must go through to get there. First, you will have to review your life; you will make discoveries and gain revelation. You will learn that you will have many options to experience your transformation. You will uncover your purpose and the hope for your future. You will make destined connections that will connect you to your purpose. You can expect many miracles along the way.

But all in all, God's plan for your success is the real driving force behind fulfilling your destiny. As you make the destiny decision to align with God and you embrace the divine design God has for your life, you will receive the reward that will radically transform your life.

Soon, you will be unstoppable!

Congratulations! You have everything you need to totally transform your life. What you have learned will move your forward on your journey to totally transform your life. Be sure to Contact me for a Free Discovery session and other powerful resources at DRLAVERNEADAMS.COM

Be sure to use this DESTINATION TRANSFORMATION workbook to chart your progress.

You have arrived at your Destination: Transformation! Now it's up to you to live a Totally Fulfilling, Pretty Amazing, Completely Rewarding Dream Life! You have everything you need to make it happen! I care about you, and I want you help you to go further than you ever have before. I have enjoyed sharing this journey together with you I hope to join you again on another journey. Look out for the other programs and projects that I have to help you advance your life.

NAVIGATE YOUR REWARD

Continue your transformation dialog and think honestly and answer these questions:

1. What do you believe is your passion in life?

2. What are some roadblocks that you think are keeping you from living a rewarding life?

3. What are your goals? What do you see yourself doing in the future?

4. Short-term?

5. Long-term?

6. Do you know why you choose these goals?

7. What is your strategic plan to accomplish your goals over the next ninety days?

8. Over the next five years?

9. How will you monitor your progress?

10. How will you celebrate your success?

Develop a SWOT assessment for yourself. Determine your strengths, weaknesses, opportunities and threats. These are my:

* Strengths–

* Weaknesses –

* Opportunities –

* Threats –

* As you answer these questions, your direction will become apparent and clear. You will begin to see the reward of your unique future unfold. The vision that you develop in your mind will be the driving force that gets you to a dynamic future. And with God's help, all of your dreams will come true!

* We can make our plans, but the LORD determines our steps. Proverbs 16:9 NLT

"Did this book help you in some way? If so, I'd love to hear about it. Honest reviews help readers find the right book for their needs." To get more info about how to leave a review, please go to:

How to Leave An Amazon Review

Look out for these other amazing programs by Dr. LaVerne Adams

TAKE THE DESTINATION TRANSFORMATION online video eCourse

Are you at a point in your life where you feel DISORIENTED & DIRECTIONLESS?

Have you recently experienced a crisis and are DISSATISFIED with life?

Do you care more about others than you do yourself?

Do You keep REPEATING VICIOUS CYCLES feeling STUCK and...

No matter how hard you try, you can't seem to BREAK FREE!

DESTINATION TRANSFORMATION is for you if...

you have tried everything else and trying to do it on your own didn't work you are ready to do the work it takes to create the life you want in life you are ready for a totally fulfilling, pretty amazing, completely rewarding dream life!

What would you do if you...

You could get a clear sense of direction for your life?

You could feel confident about your future?

You could live your best life now?

LIFE DOESN'T HAVE TO BE HARD! YOU JUST NEED THE ROADMAP

The Destination Transformation book is also the workbook to an engaging, self-guided, online coaching program that will help you better understand why your life is in the condition it is right now how you can control most outcomes in your life as well has help you learn how to be at peace with the things you cannot. You will learn how to live your life to the fullest in just 12 weeks or less! It's like working exclusively with your own personal expert coach. I've gotten everything ready for you to go on this Destination Transformation Journey to a better life! For more info, go to:

DestinationTransformation.com

Use Code: DTBOOK to get 10% Off this powerfully transformative online self-guided program.

LIFE DOESN'T HAVE TO BE HARD! YOU JUST NEED THE BLUEPRINT

Have you ever thought???

«I hate my life! And no matter how hard I try; things don't seem to get better. I desperately want to be happy Just like everyone else! I can't figure out what I'm doing wrong. I deserve better! I feel disgusted when I see others happy, but I don't want to be...I just know I need to do something about it NOW!

Are you a mature, professional woman asking yourself why????

...don't I know where to start to make my dreams a reality?

...am I exhausted from the empty feeling of being all alone?

...am I feeling like I am not enough in my relationships?

...am I frustrated because I've tried everything to be happy

...and nothing seems to work?

It's Not Your Fault!

You just need to learn the simple, proven system to build your dreams so you can wake up smiling every day because you feel so fulfilled, rejuvenated, feeling better than you've felt in years! Attract Mr. Right, & be completely satisfied in your relationships! Love your work & make more money than you ever imagined!

Attend «The Dream Life Blueprint Master Class»

This is your exclusive opportunity to have access to the only proven system that helps you get your wildest dreams out of your head into an achievable plan, so you can effortlessly create the abundant, fulling, amazing life you truly deserve and step into the next best version of Yourself!

It's Like Having a Coach for a Lifetime !

How do you calculate the value of the confidence that comes from having all the tools you need, available for lifetime access, to achieve even your most difficult goals, that can be applied to any area of your life?

I am ready to share everything I know with YOU! `~ Dr. LaVerne

Go to TheDreamLifeUniversity.com for more information about how to get started. Use Code: DLBMC to get 10% off this powerfully engaging virtual program.

BE SURE TO GET YOUR COPY OF THE
DRIVE YOUR DESTINY
Mini-Book Series

You can find all of these dynamic books and more at
<u>Dr. LaVerne's Amazon Authors Page</u>

PART I: REDESIGN YOUR LIFE

Volume 1. The Secret Key to Review Your Life - ***"Start With the Frame"***

This is your opportunity to take a good look at your life and to determine what you see as its themes, purpose, and dreams. Think about where you are and where you want to be. Prepare for the journey of a lifetime!

Volume 2. The Secret Key to Your Rediscovery - ***"What's Under the Hood?"*** -

Think about whether or not your current experiences broaden or limit you. Now think about all of the adverse circumstances in your life. Expand your thinking to the possibility that these situations exist to help you discover something wonderful about yourself . . . that you never imagined before. Get ready to make some new discoveries!

Volume 3. The Secret Key to Your Revelation - ***"Available Options"***

Think about the last time God revealed something to you. Think about the way that God may have spoken to you that you may have missed. Was it in a still small voice or through another person? Now, think about ways that you could position yourself to hear from God about your future. Be prepared for many things will be revealed to you now!

Volume 4. The Secret Key to Your Renewal-*"Remanufactured"*

As you come to this dimension you will think about your lifestyle habits and how long you may have had them. Next, you will think about the process by which these habits may have developed. Now, think about ways you can develop new disciplines that can strengthen and bring a renewal in your life. Get ready for a spring of refreshing bursting forth to wash away all the stagnant waters!

PART II: REALIGN YOUR LIFE

Volume 5.The Secret Key to Your Reinvention - *"It Had to Be Totalled!"*-

Take this moment and think the last time you changed something in your life. Think about what the change felt like and the process involved. Now imagine changes in your character, outlook, or appearance that could make your life soar. Now, get ready for a total makeover. You will be inspired to transform. You are about to be transformed in ways you never imagined!

Volume 6. The Secret Key to Your Responsibility - *"Have Car, Will Travel"*

As you approach this dimension, begin to think about the level of opportunities currently available in your life. Think about how well positioned you are for advancement or success. Think about what obstacles might be in the way of your destiny opportunities. Now, imagine how far you could advance if all conditions were favorable for you to reach your goals. Get ready! You are about to drive your way to the opportunity of a lifetime.

Volume 7. The Secret Key to Your Reason - *"The Power of Dreams"*

Take the opportunity to think about your reason for being alive. Think about what God's intended desire was for your life when God created you. Now, think about your goals, dreams, and desires. Determine that you will fulfill every purpose God intended and that you will stop at nothing until you are driven by your passion!

Volume 8. The Secret Key to Your Relationships - *"Making Electric Connections"*

Think deeply about the connections and associations in your life. Think about whether or not those relationships add to or subtract from you. Determine whether they encourage you on your journey toward your destiny. Now imagine how refreshing a mutually loving, caring relationship could be. Get ready to make covenant connections and walk in covenant agreement for your destiny!

PART III - REGENERATE YOUR LIFE

Volume 9. The Secret Key to Your Results - *"The Vehicle of the Future"*

Think about your close and distant future. Think about some of the things you would like to see happen in your life in one, three, and five year periods. Now imagine what you would need in order for you to see your future success. Move forward in your destiny and begin to drive your dreams!

Volume 10. The Secret Key to Your Reflection - ***"Feel the Difference"***

Think about what you might be looking forward to in your life. Think about the probability of these things happening. Now, raise your level of anticipation and expect the unexpected! Don't just dream it, drive it and create a higher standard!

Volume 11. The Secret Key to Your Revolution - ***"Driving is Believing"***

Think about a time that you may have experienced a miracle, no matter how insignificant you think it might have been. Think about a time that God did something in your life that you knew was out of the ordinary or defied natural laws. Now imagine that you believe that you can have experiences every day that leave you in awe and wonder. Get ready for a miracle and the drive of your life!

Volume 12. The Secret Key to Your Reward - ***"Travel Well"*** -

Think about the things in your life that make you more aware that you have a very unique destiny. Think about the course of events and themes that help you better understand the special direction for your life. You will begin see more clearly the greatness of your inevitable future. Now walk right into your destiny as you define your destiny, maximize your potential to live the life of your dreams.

DRIVE YOUR DESTINY!
Driven By Destiny
Mini-Book Series

Order TODAY!
For only $4.99 each!

⊙→ About the Author

Dr. LaVerne Adams, has spent a lifetime serving others. Born a triplet to her single-parent mother of six, in Brooklyn, New York. She knows all too well what it means to face multiple challenges and yet overcome adversity. As a result, she has a deep passion to help improve the quality of life for those who are less fortunate. She has spent decades creating safe spaces and programs serving those who have been socially marginalized. As Community Leader, Executive Director, and local church Pastor, she founded the **Motivational Achievement Program,** an educational enrichment program, specifically designed to raise the achievement levels of hundreds of underprivileged neighborhood children who were educationally disenfranchised. In 2016, she received a congratulatory letter for her 20 years of dedication for church and community service from President Barack Obama, as well as numerous grants and citations from every branch of government. She currently serves as the **Project Manager of the Ward 8 Community Economic Development Planning Process,** that is designed to collaborate community resources and educate residents in wealth building strategies to eradicate poverty and transform this severely impoverished DC community.

After being told by her high school guidance counselor that she would never be able to fulfill her dream to get into an architecture school, she applied anyway, was accepted, and went on to complete her degree in Construction Management at the **Pratt Institute - School of Architecture.** She serves others through her faith as an ordained minister and holds a Master of Divinity and a Doctor of Ministry degree from the **Palmer Theological Seminary** where she studied psychological systems theories, focusing on improving the dynamics and optimization of personal and professional relationships. Dr. LaVerne was also an adjunct professor there for over 10 years teaching Community Focused Outreach.

She has authored and contributed to over 20 books on personal, social, and global transformation including *Destination Transformation: Your Navigational Roadmap to a Totally Fulfilling, Pretty Amazing, Completely Rewarding, Dream Life*, with the foreword written by Les Brown. Dr. LaVerne is the Chief Executive Coach of **Total Life Consultancy LLC**, where she serves leaders as an Executive Coach, Organizational Consultant, and Master Facilitator, in the public and private sectors. Dr. LaVerne uses pageantry as a way to celebrate her beautifully fulfilling life as a Servant Leader. She is the innovator to the **Dream Life Blueprint Master Class** that empowers mature professional women with a strategy to get unstuck and live a life they love. And, as a Les Brown trained inspirational speaker, she has traveled extensively throughout the United States and abroad, including Africa, India, Latin American, the Caribbean, and the Philippines, inspiring thousands with her empowering message of "possibility" for a better life, a better community, and a better world. Go to DrLaVerneAdams.com for more information about how she may serve you!

For more information and speaking engagements contact Dr LaVerne@DrLaVerneAdams.com.

Made in the USA
Middletown, DE
07 August 2023

36306218R00064